I Touched the Moon!

Stories and Crafts
for Kids

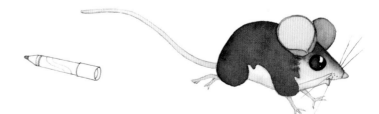

I Touched the Moon!

Stories and Crafts for Kids

Story Editor
Barbara Mains

Annick Press Ltd.
Toronto • New York • Vancouver

Contents

The Golden Goose
Story /8

Crafts /12

My Messy Parents
Story /16

Crafts /20

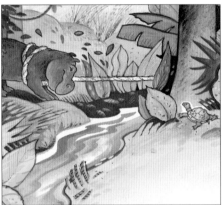

Introduction

Reading the stories is fun. Making the crafts is a giggle. Retelling the stories with homemade props is a hoot!

When storytelling and related crafts accompany reading, meaningful play and early literacy is the reward. The bonus: children and caregivers share wonderful times together, the foundations of fond memories.

Easy-to-make crafts from simple materials enhance the imaginative tales in *I Touched the Moon!* Creativity transforms toilet paper rolls, construction paper, buttons, and felt into

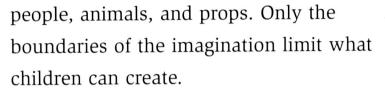

people, animals, and props. Only the boundaries of the imagination limit what children can create.

Annick Press developed *I Touched the Moon!* in conjunction with *Crazy Quilt*, a television show produced by the Canadian preschool network Treehouse TV. *Crazy Quilt* encourages young children to create simple crafts from everyday household items. Then the children use their home-made creations to retell original and traditional folk tales, fairy tales, and legends adapted from around the world.

The Golden Goose

There was once a Princess who forgot how to laugh. In fact, she couldn't even remember how to smile.

This worried the King. He ordered his courtiers to tell the Princess funny stories, and to show her fuzzy ducklings, the ones just learning to walk. The Princess listened to the funny stories, and she stroked the ducklings. But she did not smile.

Because his daughter never smiled, the King didn't smile either. Because the King didn't smile, none of his people smiled. A cloud seemed to settle over the whole country.

In the forest lived a woodcutter named Thaddeus, who didn't know that smiling had fallen out of fashion. He smiled to himself when he cut firewood for an old woman who lived in the forest, and he whistled as he carried it to her home.

The old woman thanked Thaddeus, and offered him a gift. "Which of my geese would you like?" she asked him.

"They are all beautiful geese," said Thaddeus. "The little one looks like a Golden Goose."

"Indeed she is. Now, which goose would you like to have?"

"The Golden Goose," said Thaddeus.

"She is yours," said the old woman, and went inside.

Thaddeus picked up the bird. "Golden Goose, I'll take you home with me," he told her.

Then he noticed something odd. Try as he might, Thaddeus couldn't pull his hands away from the goose. He tugged, and tugged again, but his hands remained stuck.

Thaddeus remembered the blacksmith, a strong man. "Maybe he can yank my hands free," he thought. Off he went to the village, with the Golden Goose in his arms.

"That's a fine goose!" said the blacksmith.

"She's yours if you can take her from me," said Thaddeus.

The blacksmith laughed. "That won't be hard," he said, putting his big hands on the bird. Then his face fell. "I'm stuck!" he cried. "I can't pull my hands away!"

The baker joined them. "Oh, you have a Golden Goose!" said the baker. "I've always wanted one."

"She's very sticky," said the blacksmith. "We're both stuck to her."

"I'll pull Thaddeus one way," suggested the baker, "and you pull the goose the other way." The baker wrapped his arms around Thaddeus. "PULL!" he shouted.

The blacksmith pulled the goose one way, and the baker pulled Thaddeus the other way. But although everyone was pulling with all his might, nothing was happening. Thaddeus and the blacksmith remained stuck to the goose.

"We have another problem," said the baker. "Now I'm stuck to Thaddeus!" And although the baker tried to pull his arms away, they stayed stuck around Thaddeus.

"This is ridiculous," said Thaddeus. "We need a doctor."

It wasn't easy, walking all tangled up together. Thaddeus could barely breathe with the baker's arms wrapped tightly round his waist. The poor baker couldn't see where he was going, and the blacksmith kept tripping over the baker's feet.

Then suddenly, as they stumbled round the corner, there was their King! On horseback, with the Princess and court.

"It's the King!" whispered the blacksmith.

"We'd better bow," whispered Thaddeus. He made a handsome bow, but lost his balance. The baker fell down with him, of course, and the blacksmith slid on top of everyone else.

Thaddeus couldn't hear very well at the bottom of the pile. But he did think, amidst all the squirming and the groaning and the honking, that he heard the sound of laughter.

It was a sound no one had heard in a long time, because it was the sound of the Princess laughing. The Princess was laughing because she just couldn't help it, because this was the silliest thing she'd ever seen. The King laughed until his face was wet with tears, because he was so happy to see his

daughter laughing. And the courtiers just laughted themselves silly.

When the laughter stopped, Thaddeus looked at his hands. "I'm not stuck to the goose any more!" he cried.

"Why, neither am I!" said the blacksmith.

"And *I'm* not stuck to *you* any more," said the baker, as he dusted himself off.

"There's something else," said the blacksmith. "That goose isn't golden any more."

Everyone turned to look. The bright gold had gone from her feathers, and she was just an ordinary little bird.

"I still think she's beautiful," said Thaddeus.

"We thank you," said the King to Thaddeus. "You have succeeded where all have failed. You have made the Princess laugh!"

Thaddeus bowed. "It was my pleasure, Your Highness," he said.

Then the King picked up his reins, and so did the Princess, and off they rode into the sunset.

"What will you do now?" asked the baker.

"Go home and make dinner," said Thaddeus, as he put his goose under his arm. "We're having dumplings."

Goose

Dressed-up toilet paper rolls make great stand-up figures. Or put two or three fingers up through the bottom to turn them into puppets.

You need:

**Two cardboard tubes
(toilet rolls are perfect)**
Fabric or paper: gold, white
Felt: yellow, white
Orange craft foam
Four wiggly eyes
Feathers: white, gold
Four soft Velcro dots (loops)
Scissors, white glue

Cut both tubes a little shorter. Wrap each with paper or fabric; glue. Glue on eyes.

For each goose, cut two orange beaks and two orange feet. Glue in place.

Glue a feather at top of each head.

For each goose, cut two felt wings; glue in place.

Glue two soft Velcro dots (loops) on each side of Golden Goose, so both Thaddeus and the baker can be attached to the goose.

King and Princess

Feeling creative? Decorate the crowns with paper, felt, or bead jewels to make the King and Princess look incredibly rich.

Wrap each tube with paper; glue. Glue on felt faces, then add wiggly eyes and felt noses.

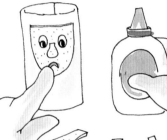

Glue a paper frowning mouth and yarn hair on Princess; glue a felt beard on King.

You need:

Two cardboard tubes
Construction paper
Felt: ivory, red, white
Four wiggly eyes
Yarn for hair
Gold paper
Scissors, white glue

Glue paper sleeves onto felt arms; glue onto bodies.

Cut a flowing felt robe for King; glue to his shoulders. Cut two crowns; glue on heads.

Old woman and Thaddeus

Wiggly eyes are fun, but you can also use buttons, paper, felt … or use your imagination.

You need:

Two cardboard tubes
Construction paper
Ivory-colored felt
Four wiggly eyes
Two prickly Velcro dots (hooks) and two soft dots (loops)
Yarn
Small feather
Scissors, white glue

Cut one tube shorter (old woman) and wrap with paper; glue. Wrap two sheets of paper around longer tube (lighter on top, darker on bottom); glue.

Glue felt face on each tube. Add wiggly eyes, felt noses, and paper mouths. Glue paper sleeves on arms; glue arms to bodies.

Thaddeus: Glue paper hat around head; add feather. Glue on belt. Glue paper ax on one hand. Glue a prickly Velcro dot (hooks) on each hand. Glue soft dots (loops) on waist at back.

Old woman: Glue on yarn hair, twisting and gluing a bun at back of head. Glue on apron.

Baker and Blacksmith

These puppets can stick together just like in the story – simply join a prickly Velcro dot to a soft one!

Wrap each tube with paper; glue. Glue on felt faces. Cut a felt rectangle for vest; glue on blacksmith.

Glue paper sleeves to felt arms, then glue arms to body.

Blacksmith: Glue on paper beard. Add wiggly eyes and felt nose. Glue prickly Velcro dot (hooks) in each hand. Glue paper hammer on one hand.

Baker: Glue on paper hat. Add wiggly eyes, felt nose, and paper mouth. Glue prickly Velcro dot (hooks) on each hand. Glue paper rolling pin on one hand.

You need:

Two cardboard tubes
Construction paper
Felt: ivory, gray
Four wiggly eyes
Four prickly Velcro dots (hooks)
Scissors, white glue

My Messy Parents

Nadya folded her pajamas and put them under her pillow. "That's better!" she said.

In Nadya's room there was a place for everything, and everything was in its place. But things were certainly different when she went downstairs.

"It's the messiest house I've ever seen," said Nadya. "Mom, could you please fold up the newspaper? Dad, could you please hang up your coat?"

Nadya knew that there's a place for everything. Everything belongs in its place, she told her parents. But unless she reminded them, her mom and dad never cleared the dishes or made their beds.

"I'm too tired," Nadya's dad would say, with a huge yawn.

"I'll do it later," Nadya's mom would promise.

One day Nadya couldn't stand it any longer.

"THIS HOUSE IS A DUMP!" she shouted. "IT'S THE MESSIEST HOUSE IN THE WORLD!"

Nadya's parents looked at each other. "You know, she's right," said Nadya's dad.

He picked up his socks, his tie, the telephone, and a bunch of bananas, and tossed them under the bed.

"We've just got to clean up this house," he said.

Then he picked up his coffee cup, his cereal bowl, his Rollerblades and two library books, and threw them in the kitchen sink.

Nadya's mother picked up her car keys and put them in her purse. "That's better," she said.

Then she opened her briefcase. It was bursting with files.

"There's never enough time to clean this house," she complained.

Gathering up the newspaper with both hands, she stuffed it into her briefcase. She was stuffing so hard that she didn't notice Nadya, who was reading the comics. Before Nadya could say a word, she found herself stuffed into the briefcase along with the newspaper.

"MOM, IT'S ME!" squeaked Nadya from deep inside the briefcase. Then she heard a click as her mother snapped it shut.

Well! Nadya had never been trapped in a briefcase before.

It was dark. It was quiet. And it was almost as messy as Nadya's house. But as she dug her way through the files and the folders, Nadya did find some useful things.

She found her favorite striped mitten. "I've been looking for you all winter!" said Nadya. "I thought you'd run away with the snowman."

Then she found one of her yellow socks, the ones she wore when she played soccer. "This is good," said Nadya. "I can always kick that ball harder when I'm wearing yellow socks."

Then—this was the best part—Nadya found the rest of the pumpkin pie, left over from Thanksgiving dinner. "I totally love pumpkin pie!" said Nadya.

She also found her baby brother.

"Max!" cried Nadya.

"Mrrng!" said Max.

Nadya hugged her brother. "Have you been here a long time?" she asked him.

Max was too busy eating pie to answer.

"I know it's nice and quiet here," said Nadya. "But I don't think we should leave Mom and Dad. They'll get into a terrible mess without us."

Just then Nadya heard another click. Someone had opened the briefcase!

She grabbed both her brother's hands. "When I say JUMP, you jump with me," she told him. "ONE, TWO, THREE, **JUMP!**"

Hand in hand, Nadya and Max jumped as high as they could. They jumped right out of the briefcase— and into their mother's lap.

"Oh, there you are," said Nadya's mother. "I was wondering where you'd gone." She smiled at her children. "I thought you must have gone to school."

"But Mom, we're too young to go to school," Nadya reminded her mother.

Nadya's mom looked surprised. "Have you seen my car keys?" she asked them.

Nadya looked around for her dad. He was outside, vacuuming the front lawn. A lot of things had been shoved under the carpet, including the garden hose.

Max pointed to a large bump in the carpet. It seemed to be moving.

"Mrrng!" said Max.

Nadya looked at her mother. "Have you seen Grandma this afternoon?" she asked.

Mother

Easy finger puppets! What could be simpler than sturdy paper people with paper rings glued onto their backs?

On scrap of folded paper, draw one half of Mother. Cut shape out.

You need:

Construction paper
Wiggly eyes
Crayons, scissors, white glue

Trace shape onto colored paper. Draw on Mother's mouth and nose; color her hair. Cut her out. Glue on eyes.

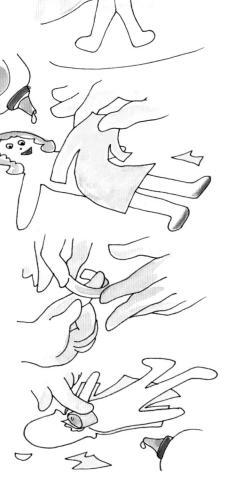

To make dress, trace around Mother's body on colored paper. Cut out and glue onto body. Color shoes on feet.

Wrap a strip of paper loosely around child's finger, overlapping the ends. Glue, then glue ring to puppet's back. Let glue dry.

Nadya

**Use a pattern to make a symmetrical body.
Draw one arm, one leg, and half a head on a folded
scrap of paper. Then unfold the pattern and trace.**

On scrap of folded paper, draw one half of Nadya. Cut shape out.

Trace shape onto colored paper. Draw on mouth and nose; color her hair, adding an orange bow. Cut her out. Glue on eyes.

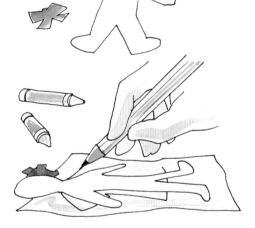

You need:

**Construction paper
Wiggly eyes
Crayons, scissors, white glue**

To make dress, trace around body on colored paper. Cut out; draw on details. Glue clothes onto body. Color on socks and shoes.

Wrap a strip of paper loosely around child's finger, overlapping the ends. Glue, then glue ring to puppet's back. Let glue dry.

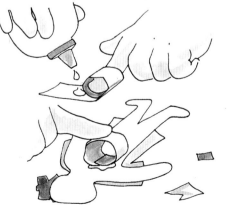

Father

You can also have fun decorating the whole family with fabric scraps and wrapping paper.

You need:

Construction paper
Wiggly eyes
Crayons, scissors, white glue

On scrap of folded paper, draw one half of Father. Cut shape out.

Trace shape onto colored paper. Draw on mouth and nose; color his hair. Cut him out. Glue on eyes.

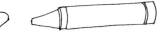

To make clothing, trace around body on colored paper. Cut out; draw on details. Glue clothes onto body.

Wrap a strip of paper loosely around child's finger, overlapping the ends. Glue, then glue ring to puppet's back. Let glue dry.

Max

Can't find tiny wiggly eyes? Try using seeds or beads, or draw on eyes with crayons or markers.

On scrap of folded paper, draw one half of Max. Cut shape out.

Trace shape onto colored paper. Draw on mouth and nose; color his hair. Cut him out. Glue on eyes.

You need:

Construction paper
Wiggly eyes
Crayons, scissors, white glue

To make clothing, trace around body on colored paper. Cut out; draw on details. Glue clothes onto body.

Wrap a strip of paper loosely around child's finger, overlapping the ends. Glue, then glue ring to puppet's back. Let glue dry.

The Mouse and the Elephant

There was once a small brown mouse who refused to believe he was a small brown mouse.

"I'm the smartest, bravest, fiercest creature in this jungle," he told the other mice. "In fact, I happen to be the smartest, bravest, fiercest creature IN THE WORLD."

The other mice laughed.

"Many creatures are fiercer than you," said another mouse, "and some are braver. What about the elephant?"

Now the small brown mouse had never seen an elephant, but that didn't stop him. "Oh, I'm a lot smarter and braver and fiercer than a silly little elephant," replied the small brown mouse. And off he went to prove it.

Right away he met a Ladybug, climbing up a dandelion. "Aha! An elephant!" cried the small brown mouse.

"I am NOT an elephant," said the Ladybug. "An elephant is much larger than I am. And it doesn't have wings, poor thing, or a beautiful shiny coat like mine. An elephant has rough, dry skin, and a tail. And its ears—" But before the Ladybug could finish her sentence, the small brown mouse had raced away.

"Got to find an elephant," he shouted.

The small brown mouse ran and ran until he was out of breath. He stopped at a large rock where a Lizard was stretched out. "Aha! An elephant!" cried the small brown mouse.

The Lizard laughed. "What makes you think I'm an elephant, you foolish mouse?" he asked.

"You're much larger than I am," said the mouse. "And you have a long tail. And your skin is rough and dry."

"I am certainly NOT an elephant," said the Lizard. "My coat may be dry, but look how the colors shimmer in the sunlight! An elephant's coat is dull and gray. He has those big tusks on either side of his nose, and his ears—" But before the Lizard could finish his sentence, the small brown mouse had run away.

"Don't have time to talk," he called back over his shoulder. "Have to find an elephant!"

All this running had made the mouse thirsty, so he went down to the water hole. There he met a Warthog. "Aha! An elephant!" cried the mouse.

The Warthog snorted. "Why on earth would you mistake me for an elephant?" he asked the mouse.

"You're much larger than I am," said the mouse. "And you have rough gray skin, and big tusks on either side of your nose. You must be an elephant!"

The Warthog rolled on his back in the mud. "Listen, little mouse," he said. "I am NOT an elephant. An elephant has tusks, as I do, and his skin feels dry and rough like mine. But he has big, big ears that flap in the breeze like the wings of a bird. And his nose, little mouse, is as long as—" But before the Warthog could finish his sentence, the small brown mouse had run away.

"Can't wait any longer," he shouted. "Have a date with an elephant!"

Around the next corner the small brown mouse ran right into an Elephant, standing in the water hole. "Aha! An elephant!" cried the small brown mouse. "You have to be an elephant, because you're so much bigger than I am. Your skin is rough and dry and gray. You have tusks on either side of your nose, and big, big ears that flap in the breeze like the wings of a bird."

The Elephant stood quietly, with his trunk deep in the water.

"You may be an Elephant," said the small brown mouse, "but I'm smarter, braver, and fiercer than you. In fact, I happen to be the smartest, bravest, fiercest creature IN THE WORLD! And I challenge you to a fight, to prove it!"

The Elephant turned to look at the small brown mouse. Then he lifted his trunk and sprayed the mouse with a shower of water and air, blowing him clean across the water hole.

"Wow! What a rainstorm!" exclaimed the small brown mouse as he landed on the far shore. "If that sudden wave of wind hadn't blown me right across this ocean, I'd have shown that elephant I'm a lot braver than him!"

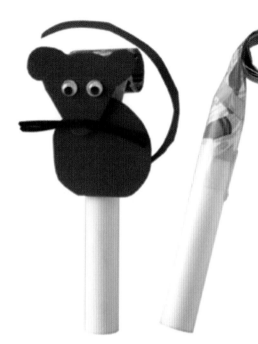

Mouse

A party blowout makes a wonderful finger puppet – the hole is just right for inserting a finger. Leftover blowouts are fun, well, to blow out!

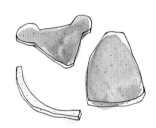

Cut out foam head, body, and tail.

You need:

Party blowout
Craft foam: brown and scrap of black
Wiggly eyes
Scissors, glue

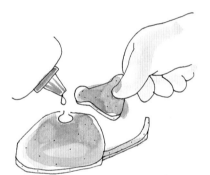

Glue head to body, then glue tail to body.

Cut out whiskers; glue in place. Glue on eyes. Let glue dry.

Glue mouse to blowout.

Elephant

Although scraps of craft foam or felt don't wiggle when you move them, they DO make good eyes if you don't have the wiggly kind.

Cut out foam head, body, and ears. Glue ears to head, then glue head to body.

Cut out trunk, legs, and tail; glue in place. Draw on toes with marker.

Glue elephant onto blowout.

Glue on eyes. Let glue dry. Cut out tusks; glue in place.

You need:

Party blowout
Craft foam: gray and scrap of white
Wiggly eyes
Scissors, glue, black marker

29

Lizard and Ladybug

Craft foam is a joy to work with (it cuts like butter), but you can also use colored paper or cardboard.

You need:

Two party blowouts
Craft foam: green, yellow, red
Wiggly eyes
Scissors, black marker, glue

Cut out foam lizard. With pen, draw on mouth. Glue on eye.

Glue lizard to blowout.

Cut a yellow foam circle. Cut fringe all around to create petals.

Cut ladybug from red foam. Draw on head, wings, and dots. Color in head and dots. Glue on eyes.

Glue bug on flower, then flower on blowout.

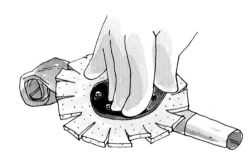

Warthog

The hardest part about making these puppets is waiting for the glue to dry! It might take as long as an hour.

Cut out foam body and legs (all one piece) and head. Glue head to body.

Cut out ear and tail; glue in place. Draw on mouth. Glue on eyes.

Cut out foam tusk. Glue in place. Let dry.

Glue warthog to blowout.

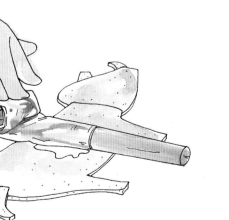

You need:

Party blowout
Craft foam: gray and scrap of white
Wiggly eye
Scissors, black marker, glue

31

I Touched the Moon!

In a faraway country there lived a spoiled Prince. He had all the toys he could want, but he wanted none of them.

One night the Prince called for the palace magician.

"What might please Your Royal Highness this evening?" asked the Magician.

The Prince pointed to the moon, shining brightly through his bedroom window. "I want to touch the moon," he told the Magician. "Get me to the moon!"

The Magician went away to his workroom, where he built a ladder for the Prince. It was one of those magic ladders that go up and up, forever and ever.

"Put your foot on the bottom rung, Your Majesty," said the Magician. "When you have climbed to the very top, you will be able to touch the moon."

The Prince shook his head. "That will take far too long," he complained. "My legs would fall off before I was even halfway there. Make me something better than that!"

The Magician went away to his workroom, where he built a rainbow. The rainbow was made of red magic and gold magic, and some other-colored magic that the Magician found in his bottom drawer. It started under the Prince's bedroom window and ended at the moon.

"Perhaps Your Majesty will find this easier to walk on," said the Magician. "See how it sparkles in the moonlight!"

"Very pretty," admitted the Prince. "But there's nothing to hold on to. And what if it disappears?"

The Magician shrugged his tired old shoulders. Then he went off to his workroom, where he made a pair of wings. They were large, strong wings, like the wings of a swan.

The Magician brought the wings to the Prince. "If the rainbow disappears, you could always fly home," he said.

The Prince put on the wings and flew around his bedroom. "This is wonderful!" he shouted.

Then he bumped his head on the ceiling. Hard. Down he came.

"I don't like these wings at all," he told the Magician. "It's way too much work, flying. All I want is to put out my hand—so—and touch the moon. Why can't you just bring the moon down to me?"

"Bet *I* can bring you the moon," said the voice of a little girl. It seemed to be coming from outside the Prince's window.

The Prince and the Magician went over to the balcony and looked into the garden. A little girl was skipping around the pond.

"How will you bring me the moon?" the Prince called to the little girl.

"Come here and I'll show you," said the little girl.

The Prince went downstairs. Then he opened the door into the garden. The little girl was still skipping around the pond.

"So bring me the moon!" commanded the Prince.

"Why, it's already here," answered the little girl, and she pointed to the pond, where the reflection of the moon was glittering in the water.

The little girl bent down over the pond. Very gently, with one finger, she touched the shining moon in the water. As she touched it, the reflection broke into ripples.

"I can do that!" shouted the Prince, and he ran over to the pond. He thrust his hand into the water and touched all the dancing pieces of moon, one after another.

"I did it!" he shouted. "I touched the moon!

I TOUCHED THE MOON!"

Then he stood up and looked at the little girl. "I don't know how to skip," he said.

"It's easy," said the little girl.

And she showed him.

Moon and Crown

Not enough buttons in your stash? Stickers, paper cut-outs, and dried flowers all make beautiful decorations for a crown.

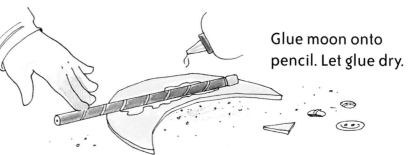

Cut out a foam moon. Glue on glitter.

Glue moon onto pencil. Let glue dry.

Cut a crown from construction paper. Glue on buttons.

Glue the ends to form the crown. Let glue dry.

You need:

Unsharpened pencil
Yellow craft foam
Heavy construction paper
Buttons
Scissors, white glue
Glitter

Ladder

Sparkling glitter transforms this tiny ladder into a stairway almost tall enough to reach the moon.

Color one side of each Popsicle stick.

Glue Popsicle sticks to pencils. Wait for glue to dry.

Glue glitter on Popsicle sticks.

You need:

Two unsharpened pencils
Five Popsicle sticks
Crayons
Glitter

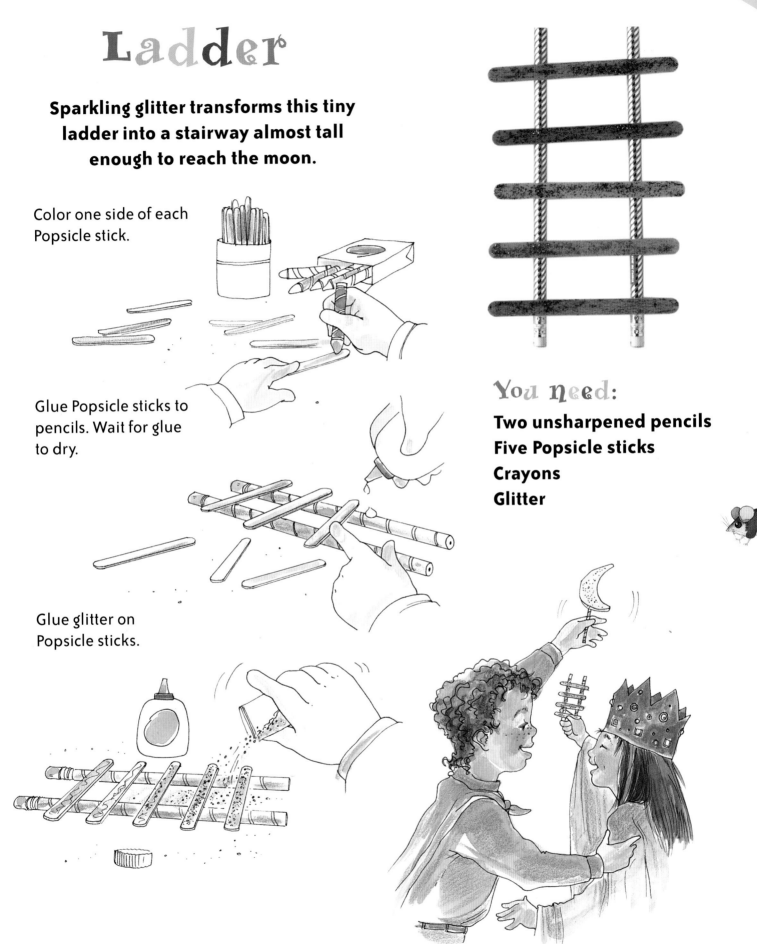

Rainbow

The pencil helps you raise the rainbow up, up, up into the sky.

You need:

Unsharpened pencil
Coffee filter or sheet of paper
Crayons: red, orange, yellow, green, blue, indigo, violet
Two cotton balls
White glue
Glitter

Color a rainbow on filter or paper. Color the sky below the rainbow.

Glue glitter on the rainbow.

Glue two cotton-ball clouds on the sky.

Glue the rainbow onto a pencil.

Let the glue dry.

Wings

Real feathers transform craft foam into magical wings.

Cut two wing shapes from white foam.

Glue feathers over one side of each foam wing.

Glue each wing onto a pencil. Let glue dry.

You need:

You need:

Two unsharpened pencils
White craft foam
White feathers
White glue, scissors

Tug-of-War

There was once a little Turtle who went down to the river to swim.

"What are you doing here?" barked the Hippopotamus.

"Oh, Hippo! You scared me!" said the Turtle. "I've come for a swim."

"Well, you can't swim here," said the Hippo, "because I own this river. No one is allowed to swim here unless I say so."

"How nice to have your own river," said the Turtle. "May I please swim in your river with you?"

"NO!" bellowed the Hippo. "If you swim in my river, I will squash you with one foot."

The Turtle didn't want to get squashed. So she went further down the river, where she ran into an Elephant.

"What are you doing here?" boomed the Elephant.

"Oh, hello, Elephant!" said the Turtle. "I thought I'd go for a swim."

"Not in this river," said the Elephant. "This river belongs to me. I'm the only one who swims here."

The Turtle thought for a minute. "You're wrong," she told the Elephant. "I am the true owner of this river, and all rivers. I will prove it with a tug-of-war."

The Elephant laughed. "What silly talk," he said.

"I challenge you to a tug-of-war," said the Turtle. "If you win, you will be the true owner of the river. But if I win, the river will belong to me, for ever and ever."

"A tug-of-war? I will beat you without even trying," said the Elephant.

"We will see," said the Turtle. "First, take one end of this long rope. I will stretch it out between us. When I yell ONE, TWO, THREE, PULL! we'll both pull as hard as we can. Ready?"

The Elephant wrapped his trunk around the rope. "Of course I'm ready," he said.

The Turtle took the other end of the rope and walked through the jungle along the river.

"Oh, Hippo," she called.

"What do you want now?" said the Hippo.

"I challenge you to a tug-of-war," said the Turtle.

"Whoever wins will be the true owner of this river, for ever and ever."

"A tug-of-war?" chuckled the Hippo. "With you? That won't be hard."

"Then take this rope," said the Turtle. "I will stretch it out between us. When I yell ONE, TWO, THREE, PULL! we'll both pull as hard as we can."

The Hippo wrapped the rope firmly around his belly. "Ready or not," he said.

The Turtle walked back through the jungle towards the Elephant. When she was halfway between the Hippo and the Elephant, she stopped behind a tree. No one could see her.

"ONE, TWO, THREE, PULL!" shouted the Turtle, and the two animals pulled with all their might.

"That little Turtle is stronger than she looks," grunted the Hippo.

The Elephant pulled and pulled, but the rope did not move. "My, that's one strong Turtle," gasped the Elephant.

The Turtle laughed as she watched the Hippo and the Elephant, heaving away at the rope under the hot sun. Such hard work!

Finally, the Elephant sank onto his knees. "I give up," he said.

At the very same moment, the Hippo let the rope fall. "That little Turtle is as strong as an Elephant," he said.

The Turtle walked over to the Elephant. "Are you ready for another challenge?" she asked.

"No, no," groaned the Elephant. "You have won fair and square. You are the true owner of the river."

"So I am," said the Turtle. "And on a hot day like today, I allow everyone to swim in my river."

"Good idea," said the Elephant.

Then the Turtle walked over to the Hippo. "Ready for another challenge?"

The Hippo shook his head. "You have won," he grunted. "I would never have believed it, but you have won the tug-of-war."

"It's too hot to play in the sun," said the Turtle. "Let's go swimming."

So they all swam in the cool blue water, floating on their backs with their toes up.

River and Tree

If you want your river to sparkle just like real water, you can substitute shiny blue paper for the construction paper. Or sprinkle on some glitter.

You need:

Sheet of brown cardboard
Construction paper: blue, green, brown
Cardboard tube
Green tissue paper
Scissors, white glue

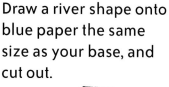

Draw a river shape onto blue paper the same size as your base, and cut out.

Fringe rectangles of green paper to look like tufts of grass. Fold the bottom edge of each.

Glue tufts of grass to underside of river.

Glue river to cardboard base.

Color cardboard green if you like.

Tree: Wrap tube with brown paper. Crumple tissue paper and stuff into tube.

Turtle

**Patience is required here –
jingle bell feet take a while to dry.**

Cut head and tail from
craft foam; glue to
pompom body.

Glue on eyes.

Cut dots from
foam and glue
onto turtle's back.

Glue on feet. Let
glue dry. (May
take an hour.)

You need:

**Green pompom
Four jingle bells
Two wiggly eyes
Scraps of craft foam
Scissors, white glue**

Elephant

These feet jingle with every step, but you can also use colorful pompoms.

You need:

**Thick sponge like those used
  to wash cars**
Four jingle bells
Two wiggly eyes
Scrap of white craft foam
**Scissors, white glue,
  Cellophane tape**

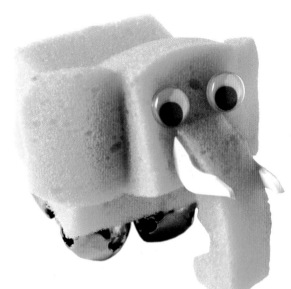

Cut body and head from sponge. Glue head to body. Wrap tape around head and body until glue is dry.

Cut two sponge ears. Glue to side of head, then fold back and glue. Hold with tape until glue is dry.

Cut tail and trunk from sponge. Glue in place and hold with tape until glue is dry. Glue on eyes.

Cut two foam tusks; glue in place. Glue on jingle bell feet. Let glue dry. (May take an hour.)

46

Hippo

While the colors of many wild animals are dull, when you make them from sponges they can be any color of the rainbow.

Cut body and head from sponge. Glue head to body. Wrap tape around head and body until glue is dry.

Cut a slit in the head to make mouth. Cut teeth from white foam; glue to mouth. Glue on eyes.

You need:

Thick sponge like those used to wash cars
Four jingle bells
Two wiggly eyes
Scraps of craft foam: white, plus two other colors
Scissors, white glue, Cellophane tape

Cut ears and tail from sponge; glue in place.

Each nostril: Glue a tiny circle of foam on a slightly larger circle; glue onto head. Glue on jingle bell feet. Let glue dry. (May take an hour.)

Treehouse TV is a trademark of YTV Canada Inc.
©2001 YTV Productions Inc., a Corus™ Entertainment Inc. Company

©2001 YTV Productions Inc., a Corus™ Entertainment Inc., Company

Illustrators
©Eugenie Fernandes *Tug-of-War* 40–43
©Vlasta van Kampen *The Mouse and the Elephant* 24–27
©Suzane Langlois *I Touched the Moon!* 32–35
©Robin Baird Lewis 1, 3, 4, 6, 7, 12–15, 20–23, 28–31, 36–39, 44–47
©Kitty Macaulay *My Messy Parents* 16–19
©Alice Priestley *The Golden Goose* 8–11

Barbara Mains — Story editor
Sheryl Shapiro — Creative director and designer

Annick Press Ltd.

We acknowledge the support of the Canada Council for the Arts, the Ontario Arts Council, and the Government of Canada through the Book Publishing Industry Development Program (BPIDP) for our publishing activities.

Cataloging in Publication Data

Main entry under title:
I touched the moon! : stories and crafts for kids

ISBN 1-55037-675-6 (bound)   ISBN 1-55037-674-8 (pbk.)

1. Tales. 2. Children's stories. 3. Handicraft – Juvenile literature.
I. Mains, Barbara.

PZ8.1.I27 2001   j398.2   C2001-930077-8

The art in this book was rendered in watercolors.
The text was typeset in Bailey Sans, Slimbach, and Whimsy.

Distributed in Canada by:
Firefly Books Ltd.
3680 Victoria Park Avenue
Willowdale, ON
M2H 3K1

Published in the U.S.A. by Annick Press (U.S.) Ltd.
Distributed in the U.S.A. by:
Firefly Books (U.S.) Inc.
P.O. Box 1338
Ellicott Station
Buffalo, NY 14205

Manufactured in China.

visit us at: www.annickpress.com

This book was adapted from **Crazy Quilt,** the craft making and storytelling series on Treehouse TV. For more crafts and stories visit **www.treehousetv.com**

Ricki Glinert — Creator and Producer of the TV series **Crazy Quilt**
Tim Chevrier — Photography
Tina Forrester — Crafts and instructions

The publisher wishes to thank Susan Ross, John Cvecich, and Heather McGillivray of Treehouse TV™.

The Golden Goose is adapted from a European fairy tale.

My Messy Parents is one of Ricki Glinert's (Creator and Producer of the TV series **Crazy Quilt**) original stories.

The Mouse and the Elephant is based on a Turkish tale.

I Touched the Moon! is based on a traditional Japanese tale adapted by Debbie Takamatsu-Stephenson.

Tug-of-War is based on a folk tale found in various parts of the world, such as Africa.